SAFE SPACE

Who We Were~Who We Are~Who We Want to Be

WRITTEN BY: KELLY ANN COUGHLIN,
DIOSPRIN PERALTA VENTURA, NIHAD RAHMAN, QUINN SANTIAGO,
NOAH SHOCKLEY, & WINNIE ZOU
~A WRITERS MATTER INITIATIVE~

Publisher's Name: Kelly Ann Coughlin

ISBN: 978-1-968442-27-9

Table of Contents

Introduction

by: Kelly Ann Coughlin

This book, <u>Safe Space</u>, is a collection of stories based around our relationship to ourselves: past, present, and future. These gifted authors are all fifth graders at J. Hampton Moore Elementary School in Philadelphia. I am lucky enough to be their Creative Writing teacher. Each part of this book was driven by their own ideas and experiences. I was not only impressed with their talent, but also with their depth, maturity, and honesty. Each piece paints a portrait of who each of these students was, is, and hopes to be. These stories are a mix of heart, emotion, and creativity, everything a writing teacher dreams of. My hope for this book is that readers are inspired to think about their relationship with themselves and how they express that to the outside world. Ultimately, we, as authors, and you, as readers, are not alone in this world; we are connected.

Who We Were

by: Kelly Ann Coughlin

"Never forget where you came from"

My dad always told me when I was a child: "Never forget where you came from". That phrase seems to flow like a river throughout every phase of my life. Kensington, a neighborhood in Philadelphia that has been known to be plagued by crime and addiction, was a tight-knit working-class community when I was a little girl. I grew up on a block where kids played until the streetlights came on and neighbors sat on their steps talking way past the time when kids came home. Brick houses lined my tiny street, and cars could only park on one side in order for people to drive down my block. To me, it was an ideal childhood: there was always someone to play with, I could walk a few blocks to school, the penny candy store was around the corner, and the playground was at the end of my block. What more could a kid want? We ran the streets playing freedom, freeze tag, run the bases, stepball, and wireball, games I thought every child played.

I never thought much about my upbringing in a comparative sense until I went to college. It was there where I realized many people who I went to college with did not grow up in a city, or go to an all-girls Catholic school, or play freedom every summer night. I was a Philly girl through and through, couldn't hide it. My "accent" was obvious to others, but not to me. For the first time in my life, I was "different" in a noticeable way. My whole world was Philly before college, and then, suddenly, it wasn't. Not everyone grew up like me. Some people's view of my city was nothing like mine. I'll never forget inviting one of my roommates over to my parents' house (my house) for dinner. She was scared to come, scared to park her car on my street, scared she would get robbed. I was astounded, confused, and weirded out. My street was certainly not dangerous. I get that some people only heard about Philadelphia on the news, in articles, or on TV shows. She didn't understand where I came from because she had never experienced living in a city. People would even say, "That person looks like they're from Kensington," as a joke to make fun of people in that neighborhood. I've never been embarrassed to be from Kensington. I'm proud to be a Philly girl, proud to have the childhood I was blessed with, and proud to be from such a cool city…at least in my opinion. I will never forget where I came from.

That theme is woven throughout chapter one in students' writing about never forgetting who or what they are from ranging from family members, cities, countries, friends, and schools. All of us are shaped by our childhood in some way or another.

Who We Were

by: Diosprin Peralta Ventura

Share the lesson and mistakes

Hey I'm Diosprin and I'm depressed! I'm writing this so you don't make the same mistakes as me in your future. So let's get started!

In 4th grade, I was wandering the schoolyard, all alone with no friends, just with my thoughts. I was entertained, but then I heard a voice asking me if I was gay. I was shocked. I said, "No (with attitude)!" It wasn't until 5th grade when the darkness crept in. The kids who asked me if I was gay bothered me so much that my blood boiled. It felt like someone reminding you of the Worst Version of yourself constantly, and one day I had it. All my friends were just sitting there staring at me in the schoolyard as I approached the edge of my breakdown; others were just helping me get through it. I told my friend to throw water at the harassers because I was too nervous to do it myself, but my friend said I should do it. I've never gotten detention or gotten in trouble for throwing water at somebody, but I couldn't help it because they were annoying me so much that I broke.

I grabbed the water and chased them. I ran as fast as I could, my legs running as fast as a supercar, as fast as an eagle striding through the air, as fast as a shooting star. I finally got close to them, I threw the water as hard as I could, and it hit them. I was surprised; I've never felt so alive standing up for myself. It's usually other people doing it, but finally, I learned a lesson to stand up for myself. And to the other people being bystanders, be an upstander next time. Standing up for yourself is another lesson to learn. Once I was called into the dean's room, I actually got scared when I was in the office. Mr. Robert told me to go find each and every one of the boys who were calling me gay and asking me if I was gay. So I did, and then we all went to the office to call their parents. "That's not true!" "He Is Lying!" They all thought that they could change his mind, but they couldn't.

So those are the outcomes of being a bully HA! Don't try me. I won't say their names, but I was going to, so I could slander their names and embarrass them, so everyone would shame them for bullying me. I want them to hear my voice saying, "You shouldn't have done that" on repeat. I hope they remember the feeling of the cold and wetness of the water that I threw at them. My only hope is that they repented for their sins. Then I will let them go from my grasp of guilt and regret. If only they apologized...

Who We Were

by: Nihad Rahman

Faith

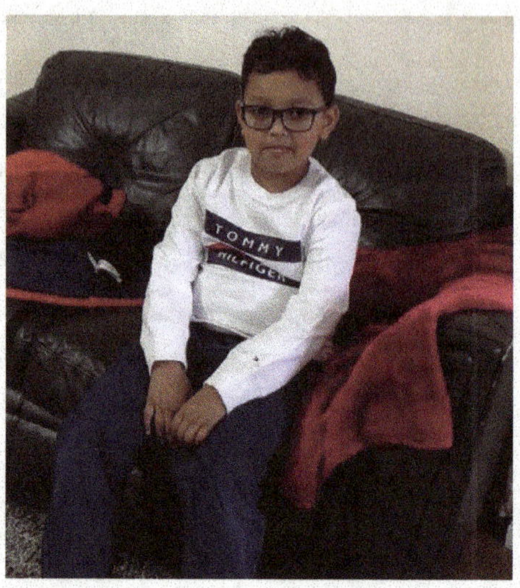

Hey, my name is Nihad. I'm a 5th grader here at J. H. Moore, soon to be a 6th grader. I was born in Bangladesh. My family and I moved to Philly when I was only four months old. My parents came here for one reason and one reason only. They came here for the sake of my future. At the time, America was known to be the country of success more than any other country. They came to start a brand new life with me.

My parents came to America, started a job, and made an average income. But for me, I wasn't the most average kid you would find on these streets of Philly. What I mean by that is I was an amazing young student for my age, a little too good. I would go ahead of all the lessons because I kind of already learnt them. But for most kids, they had a much harder time because they had no clue what was going on during class. For me, life was amazing, as I had nothing to worry about especially when I was already thriving as a young kid.

Except for my parents, it was a whole different story. Their struggles were mostly about having a hard time speaking and learning English. It's really common for most immigrants to struggle with English, so many people may understand what I'm saying. It took me many years to fully understand the struggles they had to go through.

Who We Were

by: Quinn Santiago

Memories I can't un-see

Hi, my name is Quinn. I'm a ten year old girl, and my mom and I have been through a lot together: hard times, passings, and a cluster of other situations. But nothing was like this moment in our lives.

I was in pre-K when this terrifying moment happened. Now that you know how young I was, you'll understand more deeply how scary this was for me. It was the end of the day in pre-K, and I was so excited to finally go home after a long day of having fun. My mom came in with an anxious look on her face. She rushed me out of my school and hurried me to the car. Being so young, I had no clue what was happening until I saw it with my own eyes.

I didn't cry, I didn't yell, I didn't fuss. I was just in my mother's arms, rushing towards the middle of the street. My face was looking like it was about to burst. What I saw was unbelievable. But it was real—a person lying out in the middle of the road, bleeding out of his chest. As my mom tried to get him in the back seat, I was wondering why my mom was so worried. Why would he have to sit in the back with me? I didn't know this person. What's happening? Where are we going? Little me, being so curious I asked a lot of questions. As a little kid, I thought nothing of this, but now looking back on it... this was me being brave, me being wondrous, me being curious. So scary for a four-year-old, but thanks to my focus on asking questions, I didn't worry. It would've been a lot different if I knew what was going on. I would've panicked. I would've been horrified. I would've lost control of myself.

After this incident, we never talked about it... until now. Because of that day in the car, it made me the person I am today in terms of how I look at scary things. It changed my point of view on things I should be scared of. In my eyes, things that I see on the news don't scare me as much as I think they should, all because of this. I don't quite know yet if this is a good thing or a bad thing. Maybe there might be a situation in life where I need to panic, and I won't. Maybe it is a bad thing? Now that I've finally talked about it and let it out, I feel like I released something in me that needed to come out; I just didn't know it.

Who We Were

by: Noah Ethan Shockley

Bad times turn into good times

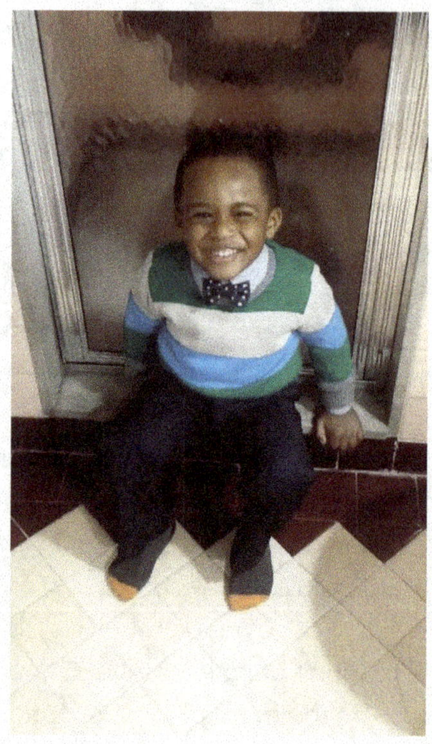

Introduction

When I was young, I went through probably the worst time of my life. During that time, I thought everything was over and my family wouldn't be the same. This little voice in my head was saying, "Everything was going to be okay," but it wasn't.... AT all! I had to make it okay, live with it, and make the changes to improve on it. I mean that's just part of who we are... right?

When I was 8 years old, I was having a normal family gathering with my mom's relatives until disaster broke out, and my uncle was on the floor from a severe heart attack. People were rushing all over the house, crying, and I did not know what to do, where to go, or how to feel. I just stood there until someone told me what to do. But at the time, it felt like I didn't know what emotions really were. Before that, I didn't know what sadness meant or what happiness meant. When you're young, every time is a good time, and then the bad times become the worst of times. I experienced that at a young age. I will never forget all the tears. I saw pure fear. So what's the lesson for telling you this sad story? Well, when we have emotions, respect them for what we are; and never, never say you can't handle them because emotions are a sporadic thing that happen either all the time or hardly at all. Even if you don't like it, bad times are the thing that makes us who we are. For example, my main goal now is to be kind and friendly to people, joke with them, and find out who they are because you never know when you will ever be able to get that moment or opportunity to do so again. That's something I wasn't able to do with my uncle, and I regret it every time I think of him. I'm not trying to scare you, but you don't know how big of a lottery we won to just be here. So let's make it worth it, am I wrong, or am I right? That's for you to decide.

Who We Were

by: Winnie Zou

Traveling Worlds Apart

Let me introduce myself. I'm Winnie Zou, a girl who currently lives in Philadelphia. I'm about to graduate from elementary school this year and start middle school next year! But before all this, I was a girl living in the southern part of Texas.

Let me rewind a little bit. I was four years old when something caught my eye, a GORGEOUS masterpiece, the toy of my dreams...a My Little Pony figurine. I snatched it with excitement and ran like my life depended on it, don't worry I paid. Anyway, I walked out of the store feeling on top of the world. I was so happy, I couldn't wait to brag to my friends about my new toy! I strutted down the aisle in style. I looked so cool holding that toy. As we pulled up to the driveway, I stuck my head out the car window to look at my boring old home. We got out of the car and walked into the house. I threw myself onto the sofa. I felt like I had accomplished a lifelong goal of mine by getting the toy I've always wanted.

As I sat there bored out of my mind, I daydreamed of things to do with my friends. But enough daydreaming because my mom was trying to make me miserable; she's calling me every 5 seconds to do something that doesn't even make sense, like wetting a wet towel. But as long as I'm not on any of the devices, she doesn't care what I'm doing. Anyway, I rushed to get my chores done so I could play later when my friends finally arrived at the house. Playing with them never got old, and I hoped that they would be my besties forever. They were the people who kept me from failing in school and stood up for me. They were my true friends. I did not know that this was all about to change.

In the winter of 2017, I had to leave Houston, Texas, to go to Pennsylvania. The new environment was harsh; city life just wasn't for me. There was too much noise, and it was so crowded. I didn't like the city; it felt like I was a bump on a log. I barely knew people, and the worst part was that I missed my friends whom I had to leave behind. I never felt so left out before. I missed all my relatives who lived there, and the family-owned restaurant we used to have to celebrate my birthdays in. I especially missed the lifestyle I was always used to, the tears I shed, and the laughter I had spread. After moving, I had to start my life all over; it was like I was starting a whole new life that didn't even belong to me. My social circle was gone and I had to accept that fact. I had to make new friends and start a new school here. I didn't like it here in Philadelphia and I thought that I never would like this place because I wasn't used to places like this. But this was reality, and I had to deal with it.

Who We Were

Reflecting on your past...

1 Who influenced you as a child?

2 What is a memory that makes you smile?

3 Think about a place that defines your childhood.

4 What is a conversation that you'll never forget?

5 What themes come up over and over again in your past?

6 If you had to choose an ideal age to be in your past, what would it be?

Who We Are

by: Kelly Ann Coughlin

I'm Not Alone

The world is a bit chaotic, a bit disconnected, and a bit sad in 2025. There are wars, disagreements, and things going on in our country that I simply do not understand. There are times when I feel alone in that thought, like I'm the only one watching the news thinking, "Wait, is this real?" Throughout the last year, I've probably asked myself that question daily. I know many other Americans have too. I've had to tell myself things will change, things will get better, and to never give up hope. Sometimes that's hard to remember, hard to believe.

One thing I know in 2025 is I'm not alone. I'm not the only one worrying, I'm not the only one angry, I'm not the only one who is cautiously hopeful. It's funny that most of my students see me only as their teacher, their goofy, smiling, singing-a-little-too-loudly, passionate Creative Writing teacher. And to them, that's who I am, the only part of me they see. I know, as a child, I saw my teachers the same way. They, well most of them, were bright lights in my day. I looked up to them, I loved them, I respected them. I didn't think of them as a woman or a man, a wife or a husband, a mom or a dad, confident or defeated, struggling or thriving; I thought of them as my teacher only.

For those wondering who else I am other than a teacher, well...

I'm a strong independent woman, it took me a while to think of myself as strong, but I think I'm getting there.

I'm a consistent worrier, sometimes about myself, a made up medical illness that I think I have, or a decision I'm not sure I should or shouldn't make. Sometimes I worry about world issues like gun violence that takes the lives of children and the lack of people who seem to care about that, or basic rights that are taken away, whether it be in speech or voting.

I'm a reader of all different kinds of books; I can't read ones that are too heartbreaking, I cry too much as it is.

I'm a lover of Christmas trees and sparkling string lights, imperfect pumpkins and cozy blankets.

I'm an avid, sometimes crazy, Philadelphia Eagles fan; I DO NOT MISS a game, no matter what is going on that day, I will figure out a way to watch it.

I'm a dog owner who was lucky enough to adopt a dog whom I love so much. I was never allowed to have a dog growing up, so having Frankie as a part of my family was a big deal.

I'm a person who has loved to hang out with my parents since I was younger. It may have seemed weird to a few of my friends who aren't close to their parents the way I am, and for that, I realize I am very lucky.

I'm a woman who feels strongly about standing up for others who are being treated unjustly, not just people I know, but also people I may never know.

I'm a person who was brought up to pay attention to what's going on in the world, to speak up when I think it's necessary, and to never give up.

I'm a person who has had times where I was extremely down and needed to accept help to get myself back up.

I'm a person who tries to see hope directly in front of me, or far away from me, but always has it somewhere in my view.

I'm a human who makes mistakes and will continue to throughout my life. I hope I recognize when I do, own up to them, and do better.

I'm a person who wishes we acted and stuck together more often than feeling like we're alone in life...because we're not alone.

Who We Are

by: Diosprin Peralta Ventura

What if I Mess Up

I'm very sensitive about friendships. I know it's not the best way to start this, but this is my chapter! I've ruined a lot of friendships, the number of possibilities can fill the Andromeda Galaxy, what possibilities you say? The possibilities to fix friendships of course! Be prepared for the future because there is going to be an explosion of figurative language, let's get into this! The code names that I'm going to use are Lili, Freddy, Nashy, and Zani. First, let's start with Lili. We get into arguments a lot, even today we still argue a LOT, and every time we did, the depression opened the door to my feelings, walked in, and made it hard to breathe. My throat would start to close, my eye shape-shifted into a waterfall, and I couldn't talk. Then, I let it all out or at least that's what I would have done, if I wasn't depressed.

I actually hold it in to not gain attention. Also if I cried, I would just hide it so no one thinks they need to help; I don't need pity, I don't deserve it, but I do hope that Lili meets some good friends in life, I know I'm not one of them.

Oh, Freddy, he's just one of my best friends, but that won't last long. I tried to talk to him, but he's got better friends who don't cry over everything. We have run out of things to talk about, but he is still a great person to have as a friend. Nashy is going to go to the same middle school as me, and that is going to save my life because I am really annoying (in my opinion). I'm still too scared to stand up for myself, AND I'M SHY. That is THE WORST TRAIT TO HAVE! It makes me feel like I'm a small mouse in the room in front of everybody, but still, she is my lifesaver. And Zani, she is the one who gives me confidence. If I get bullied, she doesn't care if it's an adult, she will stand up for me regardless. But she has better friends that she can talk to. Now, what do I do to make my friends feel good? Make them laugh like I'm a clown, or just leave them alone? What if I mess up???

If I mess up and everyone just leaves and forgets me, (warning, this part has an explosion of figurative language) I'm going to be the theoretical forgotten X planet in our solar system, or the color that you get when you mix all the colors, brown (no offense to the people that like the color brown). I feel like I don't deserve anything that I have now, why, because I treat some people like they slapped my sister badly, so have I messed up??? And what scares me is that every single move and decision that is being made alters the future leading to a different future. If I make a wrong move, those probable futures are switched to an unproblematic future, like a star supernova. It is never to be observed as a star but rather as a black hole. In other words, I could be led into a future where I could end up alone, with no friends to keep me company, to make me laugh, to.... So help me god if I end up alone, I'll just turn into a sad rainy day laying on my bed eating oreos.

This Beautiful Noise Remix Poem echoes how I feel in this chapter:

I have a voice but it's not what you think,
it's just a whole lot of
anger
depression
and sadness
clumped into a sound wave.
As they reach out of my mouth
It's like a waterfall leading into a
dark, deep, stormy sea of sound
It's a sound that can make a flower bloom.
A sound that can knock down a tree.
A sound that can shake the ground.
A sound that can call a deer
and a sound that can rip the fabric of time and space
and alter the future of someone,
Changing it
to an agonizing and recognizable end
just to let them know
I have a voice.

Who We Are

by: Nihad Rahman

Humble

Today, I'm still the same kid but academically better. I made my parents proud. I helped them with their English and they became way more successful. I'm humble and I plan on continuing that. These days at 12 years old, I'm still a young kid and have many more years until life comes to an end. By this age, there are kids that don't really focus on school and go out and have fun and enjoy their youth. For example, they ride bikes, play soccer, and play video games. Yes, I do these things too, but I like to focus on life more than just these fun things.

For me, it's the other way around, especially after all the prayers and sacrifices my parents went through. Every inch of their life was dedicated to my health and my success despite facing difficult challenges financially, mentally, and physically. As a kid, when school changes aggressively as I move into middle school, I'll have my own set of challenges in terms of rigorous assignments, being in the honors program. Much of my time will be dedicated to keeping up with the work I am given.

I will have to care for my parents and take on their roles. I do not find it fair for me to waste my privilege and opportunity I have received from these angels. I will not be wasting my teenage years outside and enjoying my youth. Instead, I would much rather enjoy my time with my parents while I can.

Who We Are

by: Quinn Santiago

Reflecting on the past

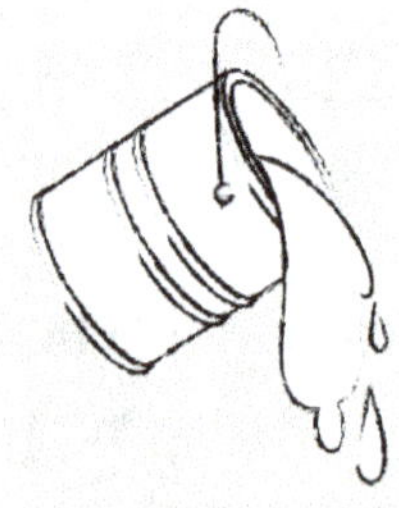

Are you scared of death? Are you scared of dying alone? Are you scared of being left behind? Maybe you are. But me… no. Witnessing someone close to death right in front of you… that scars people. It scarred me too. People don't know what I've been through. Even though many kids my age have been through worse things than me, nobody that I've met has ever said anything about it. Maybe they experienced something so traumatic that it makes them have emotions that almost make them feel like they're drowning in trauma and regret, they're drowning so deep down in the ocean where there's no light. No sign of life. No anything. It's crazy how some people have beautiful personalities, and their smiles light up the room. They are the ones who've been through the most. They understand what people have gone through, which makes them the best to talk to, and vice versa. The quietest people have the most trauma. You could walk by anyone, even someone who you think you know so well, they could be so hurt, or angered. They could've just had a bad day, but they feel down, or someone said something to them that made them feel insecure. Personally, I'm one of those people who are others' safe space. But I need a safe space myself.

I am happy. It's not an act. But sometimes… I think about things that no kid wants to think about. Ever. Hearing the laughter of other kids and funny class clowns brings light into my day. Even if I laugh so hard, I can't breathe. Sometimes I feel guilty, and I feel like I really can't breathe. I feel guilty about something I can't control. I feel like a demon is sucking my soul right from my body. There are so many things in the world to be happy about. Everyone has something that they stay for or a beautiful sight they look forward to seeing. And if you close your eyes for a little too long, you might miss it.

♡ Learn How to Love Yourself ♡

Learn how to be yourself
Learn how to love being yourself
Learn that you are enough
Learn to love that you are enough
Learn that all of the times you've failed
That you've always gotten back up
Remember that?
Remember all the times you've cried?
Remember all the times that you've been fine after that breakdown?
You need to learn that you will never be enough for one person
But another loves you enough to take a bullet for you
They love you enough to put your needs before themselves
People might not like you
But they just haven't seen the true you
They haven't seen your true colors
They don't know you like someone else does
They don't know you the way you know yourself
Even if you know yourself better than anyone else
Which you do
There's always something magical and beautiful
That you've just discovered
That you've never known
Until now...
When you enter that new world
Where you realize that the whole time you've been insecure
You just needed to look deeper into your personality

Who We Are

by: Noah Ethan Shockley

Past = Present

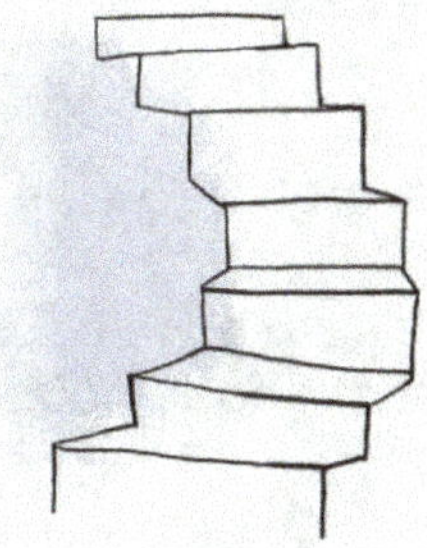

People say, let's keep the past in the past and let the present be the present. But to me, the past is what makes up the present. You see, the past makes up who we are, and the present just goes off of what we have been through... the past.

One of the main things I remember when my uncle passed was the ambulance rushing through the door, my uncle still on the floor, and my aunt trying to carry me up the steps. At the time, I could only imagine the fear and hopelessness in the room when it started. I could barely think, I was just going, and going, and going off of pure instinct. I went up the steps to the second floor and turned on the TV, trying to calm down and get back into the right mindset. I'm haunted by the fact that there's no coming back. I'm always going to remember the moment when I was an 8-year-old kid, full of excitement, and I turned into a kid who knows that life isn't all cupcakes and rainbows. There are going to be times when you're going to have to experience something that you would never dare to even think about. This moment in my life has had a big impact on the person I am now. So next time you see someone whom you truly care about, make sure that you spend as much time as you can with them.

Where I'm From

Dreams
What an odd but beautiful word
This is where I'm from
Dreaming to be somebody else
Not me
Dreaming to be seen
But yet still unseen
Dreaming to meet other people's standards
Before mine
Looking up to someone with no reason why
Telling yourself you're not good enough
Why, you ask?
No clue
And yes it's true
For years I was living a lie
I thought maybe if I did this
And did this
And changed that
Just maybe people would like me
But I was wrong
I went through sadness
And loneliness
But I dreamed and told MYSELF
You are yourself
You are
A kid with endless possibilities
A kid with a lifetime of creativity
We are all are own entity
And clearly if you put forth a little effort
Your dreams will someday turn into a reality
For all to see
My dream now is to be the best me
Not anybody else but me
I don't dream to be seen by other people
I dream to be seen as Noah Shockley
So keep on dreaming
Your dreams
And one day you will be the best you
By just being you
ONLY YOU

Who We Are

by: Winnie Zou

New Place, New Life

Currently I'm fine with my life. I mean I never thought I would like it, but now, this city life is addicting. It could be better. I wake up and look out the window and see the beautiful street I live on. My thoughts run around in my head. Not everything is as perfect as this street. I mean I never had to worry about fake friends because I've always had real ones, but things are different now. I have many best friends and a few I try to avoid. I rummage through my closet for clean clothes I can wear for school. My home can be really chaotic sometimes, especially in the morning. but I manage to find a school uniform. Even though my home is chaotic, it's just one of the traits that make it perfect for me! As I finish up my breakfast, I make sure everything I need is in my backpack.

My life feels complicated right now, so I wanna take some time to get fresh air, but I just can't find the time to do what I want. I'm always so busy figuring things out, sometimes I'm not even thinking about my own problems. I'm thinking about something else for someone else.

Currently, this is what a normal life looks like to me. I am happy with what I have. My head is always in the clouds, my imagination keeps me from going insane. I'm really lucky to have my friends. They give me a different point of view on myself. Because of them, I see myself with confidence I never had before. They help me locate all my passions, cheer me on when I accomplish something, and comfort me when I make a mistake. I wouldn't want any other people to be my friends except for them, especially my best friend. I appreciate her. If I had another hundred lives to live, I'd spend them all re-living this wonderland again.

I'm getting close to the end of this school year, and I hate to say this, but I'm gonna miss elementary school. Most of my friends are going to different middle schools. This year flew by so quickly, and I don't want it to end. It was honestly really fun. I spent the time building close friendships full of trust. The feelings I get are something I can't express with words; they mean so much to me. It gets me emotional having to think about leaving the people I love behind as I move onto another chapter in life without them.

I am from

I am from
The name Winnie which means friend of peace
It really describes who I am and who I try to be
I am from
Putting a smile on your face
This doesn't have to be a race
I am from being your friend
If not today, then tomorrow
You get the memento
I am from helping out the community
And having the opportunity to work with different people
Of different races
Meeting new faces
everyday
I am from a loving heart
I'll do my part
I'll fix what you need
Because
I'm a friend of peace

Who We Are

1 How do you see yourself?

2 How do others see you?

3 Who is a person in your life you would like to have a conversation with?

4 Who or what is making you happy now?

5 What is something you are proud of?

6 What part of yourself would you like to show more of?

Who We Want To Be

by: Kelly Ann Coughlin

An Adventure Awaits

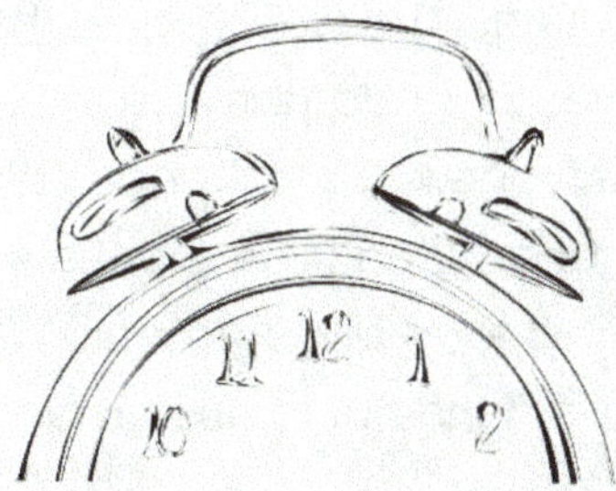

You know that saying, "Life is an adventure," well, that's not really my vibe. I'm not an affirmation saying kind of gal...but maybe I should be. Recently, I started thinking about my future in terms of...what kind of adventure can I go on? When I say adventure, I don't mean hiking Mt. Everest or swimming with sharks in the Atlantic or diving out of a plane with a parachute attached to me. I mean, not knowing what might come next and being okay with that. I want to explore places, things, and possibilities. So, I plan on calling myself an adventurer and an explorer, not like Lewis and Clark, surely not like Columbus. Maybe a little adventure will happen when I walk my dog; I will venture off on streets and neighborhoods I may have never walked through to do something different, see something different. It doesn't have to be monumental, but may be something unexpected. Maybe I'll explore new countries in Europe, hike a not-so-tall mountain somewhere, stare at an otherworldly waterfall in Iceland, or sit at a cafe on a small street in Italy staring at the beautiful old buildings surrounding me. That's the future I'm hoping for, pushing myself to continue to think about things a little differently than I have in the past. I'm a person who gets bored with monotony; some need that. I'm a daydreamer, always have been.

The other saying, "You never know what you might find around the corner…" may prove to be true. Life is weird sometimes, well, most of the time. Sometimes things work out how you thought they would, sometimes things don't. Then, there are the parts of life that are surprising, unexpected. It's in those moments, those minutes, those seconds, that time stands still. Your heart or your brain becomes a statue, and time stops for a bit. The thing about time is that it keeps going with or without you. I want to be there when time moves on, as I grow older. I don't want my mind to always go back to the past. We all struggle with that; it's hard not to as humans.

Starting today, I want my suitcase to be filled, I want my train to be ready, I want my body to be healthy, and I want my mind to be sharp. The future is scary and unknown. It's like a tunnel, a tunnel is dark for a bit, but there's always light at the end. The past will forever affect our future; that is a truth that cannot be argued. However, the future is just like the night sky, stars may be dim or burnt out, even, but they still shine brightly for all to see. I plan to walk into the adventure of the future, the unknown, knowing that it will be a memorable one, and hope to shine bright, to not burn out, and to allow all to see me for all that I am, and was.

Who We Want To Be

by: Diosprin Peralta Ventura

Feelings and Thoughts

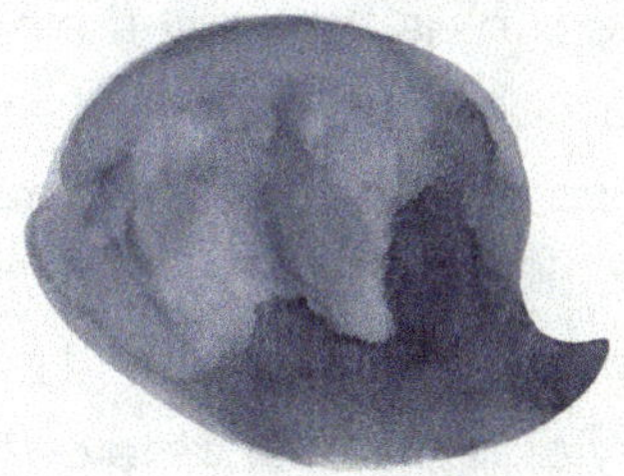

Everyone has bad thoughts and bad feelings, even people that act happy sometimes have bad thoughts, like me. I act happy just to see others happy, it's kinda one of my life goals. It's hard for me to see other people in the state that my mental health is in... BAD. That's one reason why I don't speak my mind. My bad thoughts affect my feelings, feelings affect my words. It's like I'm a puppet being controlled by strings and the controller is my depression, though it only pulls the strings when I'm around everyone else. And to be like this in my situation is worse than the definition of bad. I get bad thoughts about myself every day: "Give up" or "You're worthless". If I put my other thoughts in here, I might get taken away to a mental hospital, fearing if I make a wrong move in life I might go down to eternal burning. I'm thinking about that every single day! "What if I do this? Is it ok with god? No! I shouldn't do this!" Thinking about my aunt who passed and that at the same time is worse.

Another thing is I feel like I stand out too much, I look like a girl but I'm actually a boy, wait am I A BIRL? I stand out like a dwarf planet, something that's not great enough to be something else. But, I can have good thoughts sometimes! So that means there's hope! And seeing everyone happy makes me happy! "But you aren't," says Depression as they put their hand on Diosprin's shoulder. "In life, everyone can't have what they want to have, and everyone can't be who they want to be. You could end up a successful musician, or you could end up in the dark, alone, with no one to support you." Darkness starts to corrupt Diosprin's room, then strings fly at him. Seconds later, the strings snapped in half with an explosion of light and colors. "What? HOW!?!" "You know, I thought you would know me," says your depression, "but I guess you are dumber than I thought because there are so many possibilities for me if you don't control me." Depression's eyes start to tremble in fear. "A-and how are y-you going to stop me?" Diosprin tilts his head, a shadow lays upon his face.

The strings were tied back together in a flash, then they flew toward Depression and connected to its limbs so it couldn't move. "I will become a successful musician so I can provide for my family and friends who need it. I will make everyone happy with the sound of my bow sliding against the strings of my cello, creating a beautiful noise. This will be the best part of me. I will be the person who will reinvent something that is ugly to be beautiful. It won't be easy, but I WILL ACCOMPLISH MY DREAM!" Diosprin's eyes glow white with happiness. "No, YOU CAN DO THIS DIOSPRIN, PLEASE WAIT!" A wormhole-like portal opens up behind Depression sucking him into the dark realm behind it then fading into dust. "Diosprin La cena está lista, ven aquí para que puedas comer." Diosprin's mom is calling him down for dinner, so Diosprin walks down with attitude and sass A.K.A. confidence.

The Opposite

By: Diosprin Peralta Ventura

Hate Can turn into love
Shame Can turn into pride
Don't live in the shadows
Go out in the open
Depression Can turn into blissfulness
Sadness Can turn into happiness and
Sin Can turn into a kind deed
If you give someone kindness
You deserve it too
A scribble Can turn into a drawing
A seed Can turn into a tree
Everything ugly or scary on the outside
Can be beautiful and lovely on the inside

Who We Want To Be

by: Nihad Rahman

Sabr (Patience)

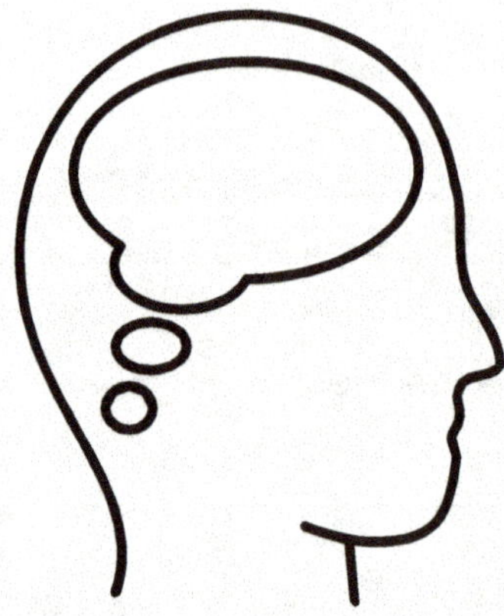

Some patterns go on for generations and generations but for me getting put into a different world of advanced technology makes me think I can break the pattern of worrying about money. I know I want to make the next generation of my family go from middle class to upper class. I know that making a whole new generation different will take lots of risks and sacrifices, but I know I can do it if I put my mind to it. There will be a lot of temptations. For example, I may be stressed about not getting accepted into another company's investment. Things like that could take my business diving to the ground. There may even be a time where I would leave my family for something important like marriage or anything like that may separate me from my dad's motivation. In the blink of an eye, I'm alone. There may be a time where life comes down. But my motivation to stay consistent is about my dad. I feel like there's never enough love and respect to repay him.

In Bengali culture, no matter how old you are, you're always supposed to respect your elders and take care of them once you become an adult. Some cultures may not be the same as mine. Or even my own people may not follow this rule, but I will, which makes me different from them when it comes to maturity; and that's what I live for.

This is a "Beautiful Noise Remix" poem that sums up my love for my parents.

I'm not living to die
I'm out here tryna retire my mom.
I wanna hear her break down in total tears
Telling me how much she's proud
Started out a whisper, turned into a scream
I was depressed at first but stood up for myself.
I have a voice and look where it took me.
Look at my mom, she admires me.
Look me in the eye.
Tell me I did it, Tell me I did it
Tell me I successfully retired the person
That brung me into this world
Then I can finally sleep.

Who We Want To Be

by: Quinn Santiago

Nobody knows

Who will I be? Where will I go? What's going to happen in the future? Who knows? But I know what kind of person I want to be. I want to achieve what I believe and help others believe in themselves, too. I don't know what job I want to do yet, but I'm considering a career as a therapist or a veterinarian. But either way, I want to help someone. Being a veterinarian can benefit both the animal and its owner. Being a therapist, I can help people overcome fears that they didn't even know they had. There are probably other jobs out there that can help people physically, like a doctor. But I can't commit to something like that. Having someone's life in my hands...No. I'm not the right person for that. I'd feel so guilty if I were working so hard and the patient didn't make it. I would feel bad for the person who had to tell them that their loved one didn't make it, but mostly for the family. I know what it feels like. It's terrifying to know that that could happen to anyone, anywhere. It's hard to think about how so many people in the world have to experience that feeling.

Where will I be?
What will I be?
Who will I be?
Nobody knows.
But I know where I want to be
I want to be somewhere where someone loves me.
I want to be somewhere where I feel safe.
I know what I want to be
I want to be someone who overcomes her greatest fears.
I want to be someone who knows that I'm enough.
I know who I want to be

Who We Want To Be

by: Noah Ethan Shockley

Unfinished Project

So after the last two chapters, you heard about my experience with my uncle's passing and how it impacted my life. This last chapter of mine is going to be about how it will also impact me in the future.

I know the world around me may get worse, but my goal is to be a leader and change the people around me from being under the biggest influence in the world......the world. My name is Noah and Noah means comfort and a peaceful mind, I think that I was given that name for a reason. For instance, in life, rocks might hit you and they may feel like asteroids, but that's all in your head. If you take it and get back up, then it will feel like a pebble ...you know. So next time when I get knocked down, I'm going to get back up however long it takes. I want to build on my losses, my mistakes, my tragedies. I'm going to make that negative turn into a positive. And that is something that a lot of people can't do or just don't know how to. Where I'm going is still unsure or unseen huh... I got an Idea. If this paragraph didn't speak to you, then I hope this will. I hope...

Where I'm Going

Where I'm going is unseen
I hope this is only for you and me to see
I hope this hits you deep
Just how badly it worries me
I don't know what I'll be
This is my biggest mystery
But this is not a case to be solved
Because my imagination will not dissolve
My name is Noah Shockley
A kid with endless possibilities
But the change I WILL have on others will not be unseen
I will make sure I impact lives
For you to see
This is not where I'm going
This is where I hope to be
I hope someday someone will look back at this and say
Wow, this kid made history
I don't care if I'm the poorest or
The richest man in the world
I'm going to be me
For all to see
I could think for hours
About what I would want to be
But there is no real answer
To this equation, there's no sum to be seen

This is a life of monopoly
You can win, you can lose
There are no rules
It's just about what I want to do
But I will not live in fear
Because the end of this poem is near
For this kid's legacy
Is just like the fog and shadows
It's unclear
I don't know if it's even near
But don't worry, this is just another case
A mystery, with no what
No why
And no where
Where I'm going is unseen

This journey with you guys has been bumpy, but also one of the
best and I hope you enjoyed it just as much as I did.

Who We Want To Be

by: Winnie Zou

Life Changing Decisions

I never knew coming here, to Philadelphia, would have such a huge impact on my life. Everything changed for me. In Texas, I thought I knew what I was doing, where I was heading. I had so many people to argue with that when I discovered you can be a lawyer, that's what I wanted to be. I wanted to argue against people and win cases. That job felt like a win for me. It felt easy and it sounded fun. But when I moved here, I had less people to argue with because they all became my friends so fast. Everything fell into place so quickly, I didn't want to argue with people anymore, and I didn't want to be a lawyer anymore. Now don't get me wrong, being a lawyer still sounds awesome, but it's just not my vibe anymore.

Now, I see myself as a college professor teaching young minds to work towards finding the right path that they belong in. I want to see people succeed in what they are best at and celebrate big achievements. After moving here, my love for education deepened, and my love for school flourished. My teachers taught me everything I needed to know so I wouldn't fall behind. For the past two years, I have dreamed about being a professor, and one day I hope I will make it as one. I want to be a professor that people will remember, not for a bad reason, but for a good reason. I want them to remember me as a professor who believed in what path they chose to take and who helped them day by day. I want them to know how much time I put into my job and how many things I would sacrifice for them. I never even thought about being a professor until my friends, mom, and dad made me believe that I could have potential, so huge thanks to them. I am really thankful for the fact that I have true friends and parents who believe in me. Without them, I would have never known what I wanted to pursue in life. I know that I might not make it big, so my goal is to help other students achieve what I couldn't. Through the highs and lows, I vow to fill my role as a teacher as perfectly as possible! Personally, I think people can pursue their dreams if they try instead of acting clueless which is why I want to push students to their limits. That is why I want to be the one who pushes them to do the most.

Who We Want To Be

Reflecting on your future...

1 What do you see in your future?

2 What kind of person do you want to be?

3 Is there something you're doing now to prepare for your future?

4 Who are the people you hope are part of your future?

5 What advice would you give your future self?

6 What adventures do you hope to go on in the upcoming years?

About the Authors

Kelly Ann Coughlin is a Creative Writing teacher at J. H. Moore. She's a passionate educator who gets a little too excited about projects that involve imagination and creativity. She has loved writing since her teacher gave her a prompt in third grade that began: If I had a pair of magical glasses... She's goofy and sings A LOT in class, especially kindergarten ones. She is obsessed with design whether it be Google Slides, living rooms, buildings both inside and outside, and fashion. She loves listening to jazz with a cup of tea in her hand. She loves being around her family & friends. Her sidekick is her dog, Frankie, her best friend. She loves, feels, and thinks a little too much. She will always be filled with hope.

Diosprin Peralta Ventura is a person who creates good possibilities for themselves and others so fast like how a race car zooms past a butterfly. They make poems about life and stories about the night, and even though the dark is tragic, the light is magic. Their favorite color is blue like the sea and black like the night. They studied at J. H. MOORE for almost 5 years. Their dream is to be a musician; they play the cello for happiness and for the sound. Diosprin has been studying music for three years at J. H. MOORE and by the time this book comes out, they will be in 6th or 7th grade. Special thanks to their turtle, Pebble, for giving them the confidence to write about their feelings.

About the Authors

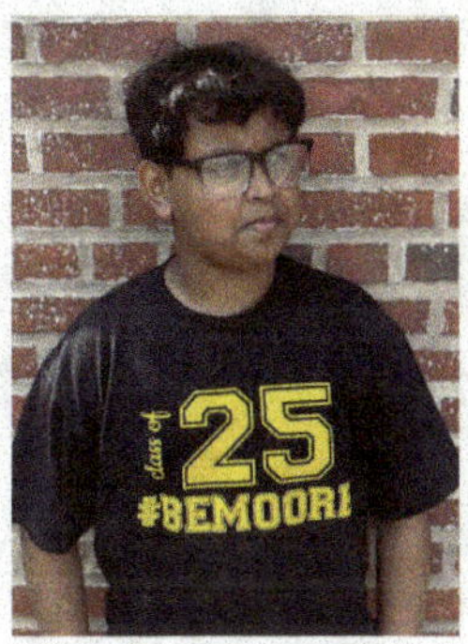

Nihad Rahman is a 5th grader at J. H. Moore. He's talented in writing class. His main hobby when he was younger was playing with Hot Wheels cars; it was his whole life. He realized this was his passion. His main priority is his parents, and that is who he writes about. He's kind and likes to be on people's good side. But when you get on his bad side, chaos erupts. He's a good example of maturity and humility to kids his age.

Quinn Santiago is a 5th grader at J. H. Moore. She is talented in writing poems, she realized that writing was her passion. She has a beloved cat and the best mom that any kid could ever ask for. A rude person when she has to be, but a sweetie at heart. Someone who smiles for others but not really for herself. Someone who cares a little bit more about being pretty on the outside, but not the inside. She wishes to grow up soon, but knows that she'll regret it later. She found light at the end of the dark tunnel. The light for her is writing. It's easy to let out feelings in writing instead of talking out loud.

About the Authors

Noah Shockley is a former J. H. Moore student. A kid with a wild imagination. He wishes to be an electrician one day and let his imagination help or build homes. He is a die-hard Philadelphia Eagles lover. But this bio is who he is, and he wouldn't be anything without his family. Those loving and caring feelings they show him are something with no price tag. He is also a kid who would like to imitate his dad and have a family of his own. He is also one of Jehovah's Witnesses and that pushes him through whatever trial battle he is going through. But all in all, I hope you enjoyed his part of this book or will enjoy his part of this book and everybody else's. He hopes you have a great rest of your day and what J.H. Moore likes to say is: BEMOORE.

Winnie Zou is a girl who learns at J. H. Moore, with a big attitude and a big heart that comes with it. She is passionate about music and writing. A person who loves to indulge in beauty. A person who values others over herself. Her biggest goal is to find true friends she can share good memories with. She hopes to one day make it big in life, but she knows reality will have different plans for her. She's a girl who loves to make serious situations into goofy ones and does nothing but laugh.

Acknowledgements

This book would not have been possible without the constant encouragement of Dr. Bob Vogel, the founder of Writers Matter. When Dr. Vogel asked me to choose students to write a book, it was an absolute honor to create something with a group of fifth grade writers. Never did I imagine what this project would bring us. A tiny crew of writers meeting in a small hallway table weekly turned into a family of artists creating pieces that not only inspired each other, but hopefully will inspire others. Writers Matter has been an organization I have been part of for many years. It's a constant source of encouragement and inspiration. I hope everyone has a mentor like Dr. Vogel, someone who not only looks out for teachers and students in Philadelphia, but to those around the world. I am eternally grateful for this opportunity.

-Kelly Ann Coughlin

A Writers Matter Initiative
www.writersmatter.org

TREE OF TIME

Time grows like a tree,
you need to make memories for time to grow
but you need to give water to a tree for it to grow too.
Everyone's timeline is a tree
and every branch on that tree
is a mistake, a heartache, a bad memory,
all that good stuff
but there is always hope for time
because everyone has good memories
so when leaves grow,
It means you're doing the right thing
and making new friends
and good memories make the tree
big and bright with greenery
when your time has come to pass on
your tree stops growing,
but don't be sad
the tree lived a happy healthy nurturing life.

www.ingramcontent.com/pod-product-compliance
Lightning Source LLC
Chambersburg PA
CBHW071215300726
48975CB00004B/1316